LIVING IN SPACE

Carmel Reilly

Australia • Brazil • Japan • Korea • Mexico • Singapore • Spain • United Kingdom • United States

Living in Space

Fast Forward
Silver Level 24

Text: Carmel Reilly
Editor: Cameron Macintosh
Design: Ami Sharpe
Series design: James Lowe
Production controller: Seona Galbally
Photo research: Fiona Smith
Audio recordings: Juliet Hill, Picture Start
Spoken by: Matthew King and Abbe Holmes

Acknowledgements
The author and publisher would like to acknowledge permission to reproduce material from the following sources:

Front cover: Corbis Australia Pty Ltd
Back cover: iStockphoto/Joshua Smith
Corbis Australia, pp 4, 15, 23; Getty Images, p 9; Getty Images/AFP, pp 3, 14;
Photolibrary, p 5-8, 10-3, 16-8, 20-2; Jupiterimages Corporation © 2007, p 19.

ISBN 978 0 17 012711 0
ISBN 978 0 17 012705 9 (set)

Cengage Learning Australia
Level 7, 80 Dorcas Street
South Melbourne, Victoria Australia 3205
Phone: 1300 790 853

Cengage Learning New Zealand
Unit 4B Rosedale Office Park
331 Rosedale Road, Albany, North Shore NZ 0632
Phone: 0800 449 725

For learning solutions, visit **cengage.com.au**

Printed in Australia by Ligare Pty Ltd
7 8 9 10 11 12 13 20 19 18 17 16

Evaluated in independent research by staff from the Department of Language, Literacy and Arts Education at the University of Melbourne.

Living in Space

Carmel Reilly

Contents

Chapter 1

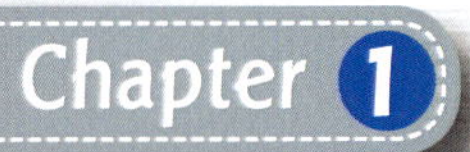

THE HISTORY OF LIVING IN SPACE

Space travel is nothing new. The first spacecraft with a human on board blasted into space in 1961. Since then, people have not only been travelling to space, but many of them have also lived there for extended periods.

The Soviet Union (Russia) launched the first space station in 1971. This space station was called Salyut 1.

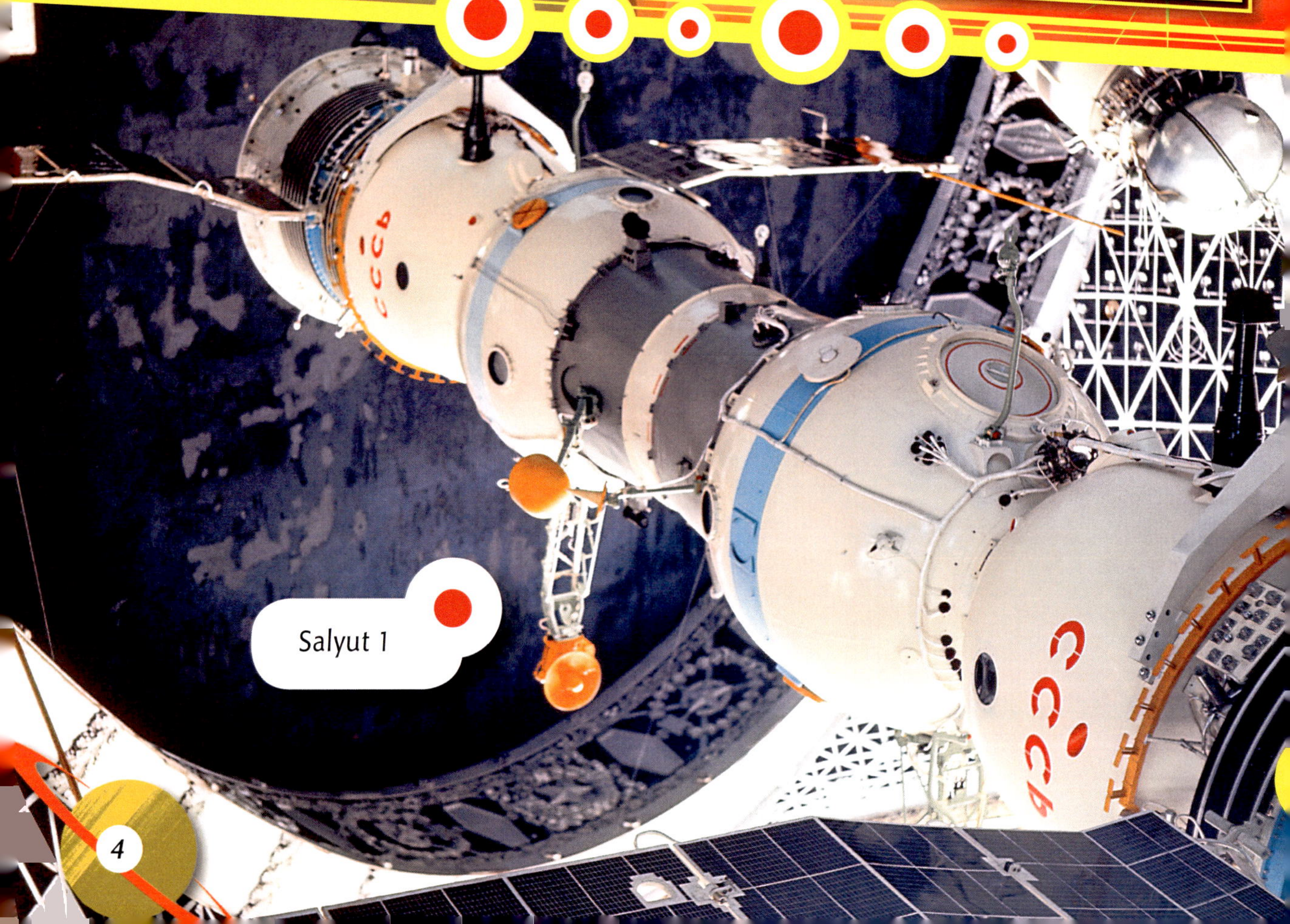

Salyut 1

Salyut 1 was designed as a place where people could live while they made observations and conducted experiments.

Russian cosmonauts on their way to Salyut 1

The first crew of cosmonauts (the Russian term for astronauts) arrived separately in a spacecraft and docked with the space station. Then they entered Salyut 1 and lived there for 23 days. While they were there, they conducted experiments and observed space and the Earth below.

The Soviet Union went on to make seven more Salyut space stations. At about the same time, the United States launched its own space station, called Skylab.

Crews visited and often lived on these space stations for short periods of time. However, it wasn't until the late 1980s when the Soviet Union launched the Mir space station that people began to live in space for extended periods.

Mir was inhabited continuously from 1989 until 2001, when it was decided that the space station was too old and no longer safe to live in.

Russian cosmonauts (wearing light blue) meet American astronauts in the Mir space station.

Running Words 214

astronauts Susan Helms and Janet Kavandi inside the International Space Station

However, a permanent two-person crew now inhabits the International Space Station. The International Space Station was launched in 2001 and is still being built. Over the next few years, it is expected that larger numbers of people will live and work there.

Chapter 2

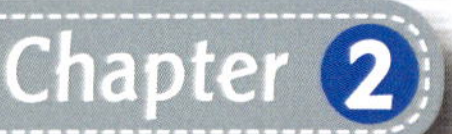

PREPARING TO LIVE IN SPACE

A lot of organisation goes into living in space. Astronauts have to begin preparing themselves physically and mentally for the trip, long before they blast off from Earth.

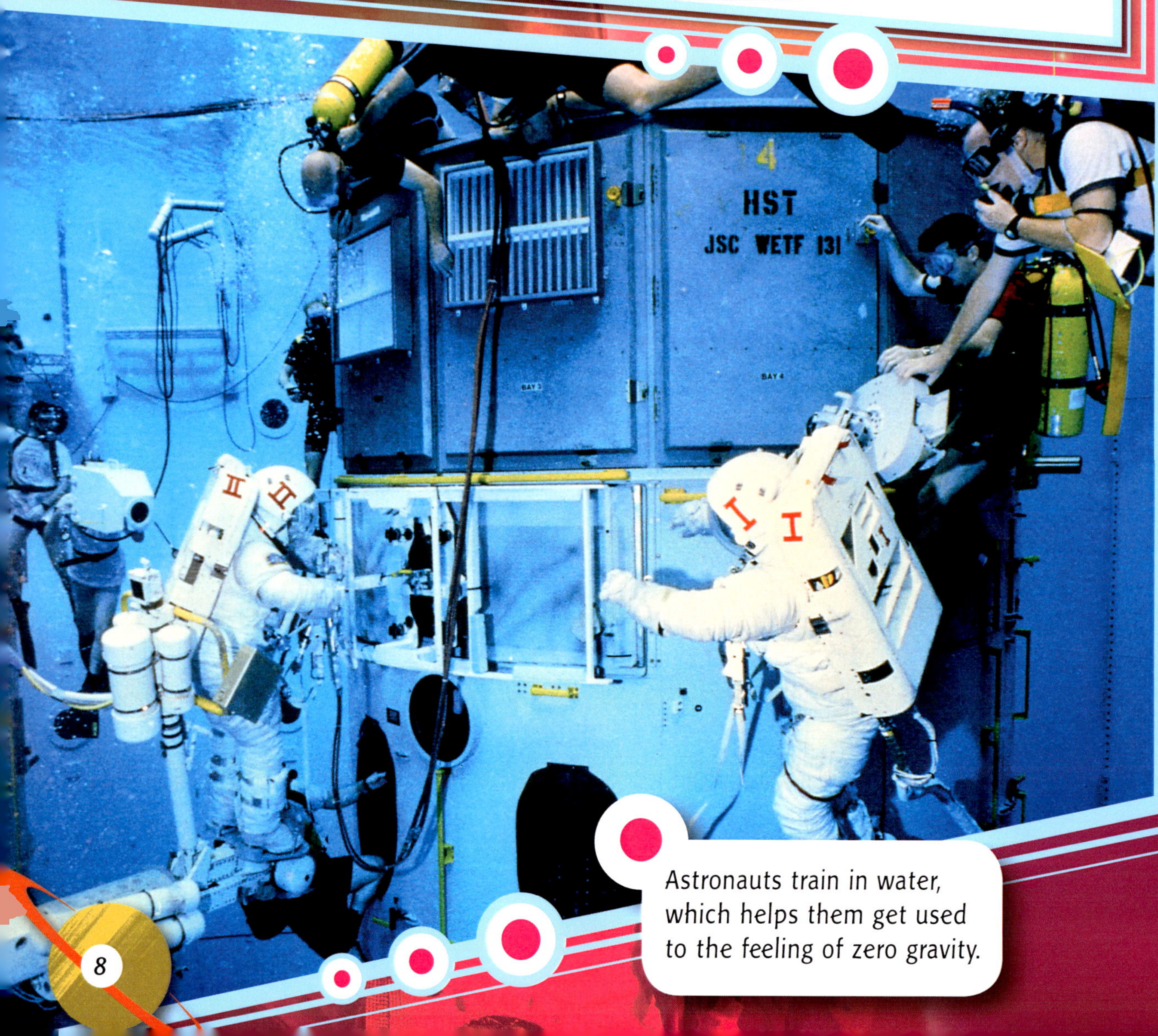

Astronauts train in water, which helps them get used to the feeling of zero gravity.

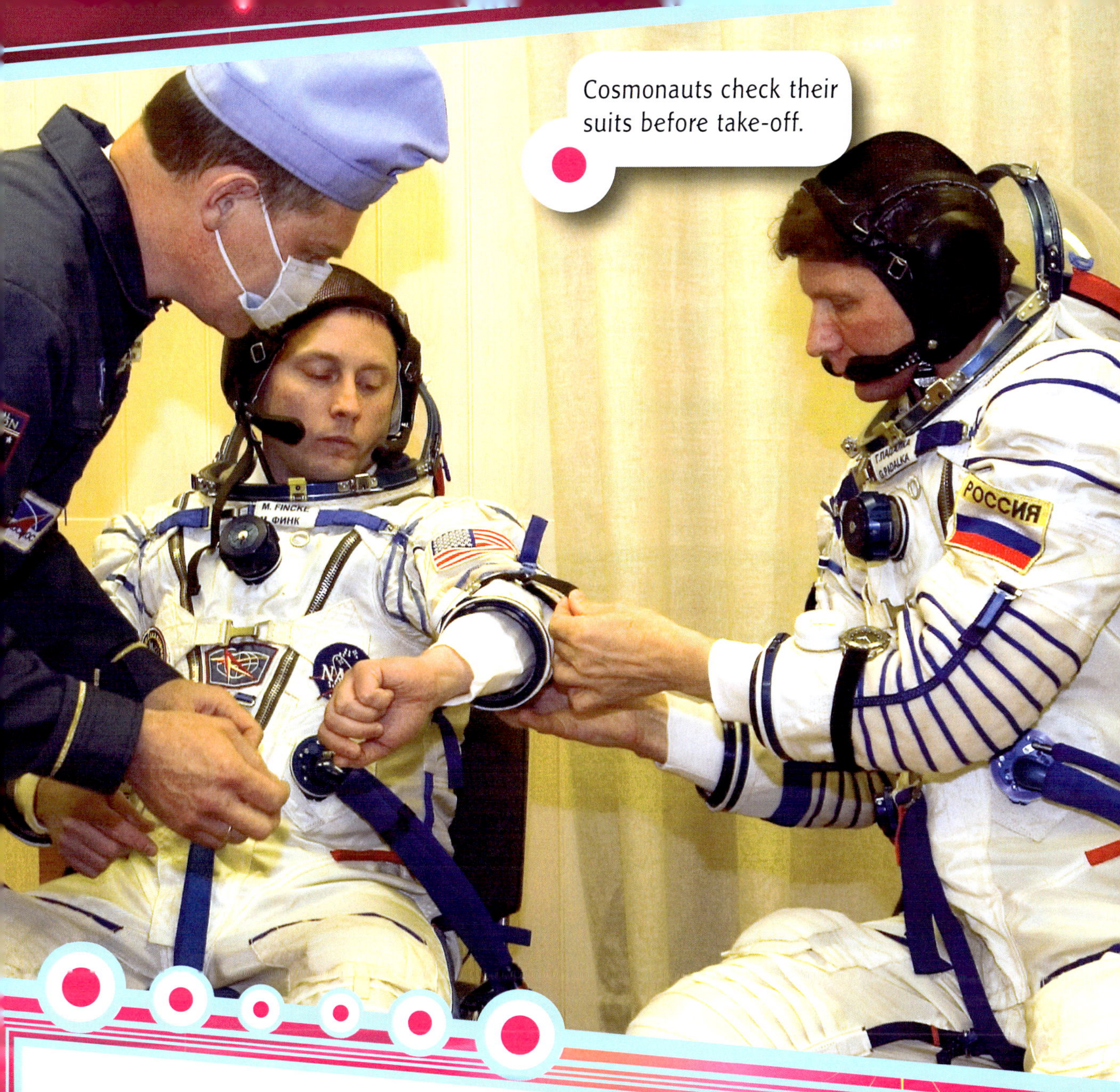

The ground crew also has to prepare everything for the trip. All the meals are prepared. The astronauts' medicines and any other needs have to be organised. Everything that the astronauts will need for experiments needs to be planned for. Bags have to be provided for all rubbish and human waste materials.

Chapter 3

ON BOARD

There are many things that make living in space very different from living on Earth. Crews of space stations must cope with:

- microgravity (very little gravity compared to Earth)
- a small area to live and work in, with no outside area for recreation
- living and working with the same person or people for months on end

astronauts Lee Morin and Ellen Ochoa inside the International Space Station

- a highly structured and organised daily routine
- an environment where the air and water has to be constantly recycled.

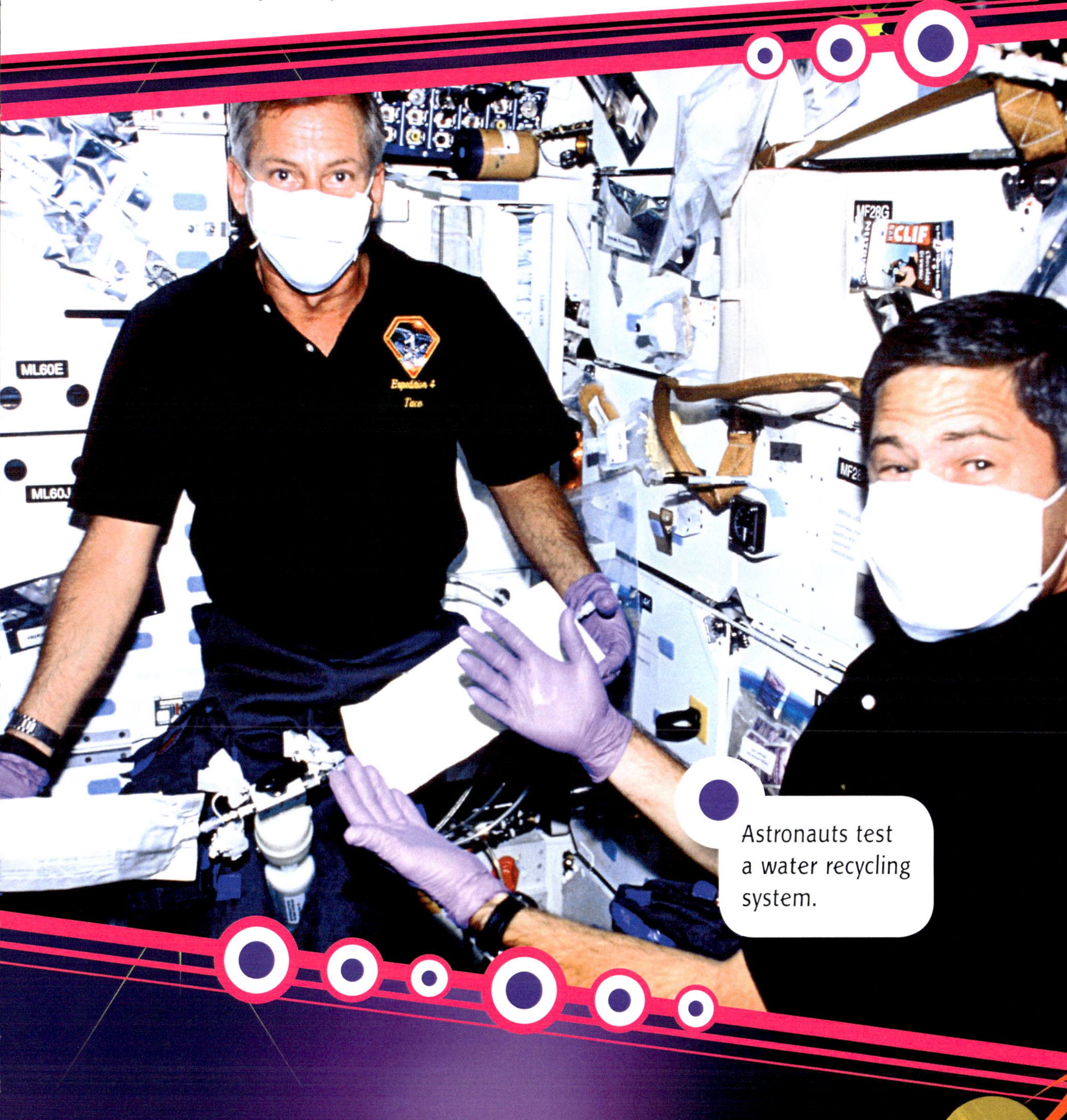

Astronauts test a water recycling system.

Chapter 4

WORK

A few people have visited space stations as tourists, but most people visit space stations to work. The crew on board is expected to conduct experiments and make scientific observations. Each day is well organised, with time put aside for each astronaut to do special tasks. Many of these tasks centre around running the space station.

Astronaut Peggy Wilson checks the plants growing inside the International Space Station.

The crew is expected to check air and water, keep everything clean, and fix anything that is broken. The crew members need to be able to work well together so they can get all the tasks done quickly and easily.

Chapter 5

FOOD

All the meals on space stations are put together on Earth and sent to the space station, along with the astronauts, by space shuttle. Because the food has to last a long time (sometimes up to three months), a lot of it has to be preserved by **dehydration** or **canning**.

instant "space noodles"

The space station does not have a freezer to preserve food, but it does have a cool room to keep fruit and vegetables fresh.

Astronauts also eat many other foods such as cereals, cereal bars, nuts and dried fruit that do not need any special preparation.

Eating

Astronauts have a set timetable each day. This tells them when to do everything, including when to have their meals. At meal preparation time, they start getting their food ready, which often includes adding water to re-hydrate the dehydrated foods.

Astronaut Thomas Akers re-hydrates some fruit juice.

Without the help of gravity, sitting down to eat can be tricky. Astronauts sometimes have to strap themselves and their food into place. Because of lack of gravity, astronauts cannot use ground salt and pepper, and all drinks must be taken from bottles. They also have to be careful that crumbs do not fly off and get stuck in vents and instrument panels.

Chapter 6

REST

Microgravity makes sleeping on board a space station difficult. In order to stop themselves from floating and bumping into things when they're asleep, astronauts have to tie their sleeping bags to their sleeping bunks. The constant movement due to lack of gravity can also give them motion sickness.

Sleeping on the space station is also difficult because the station **orbits** the Earth 16 times a day. This means that the station moves through day and night every 90 minutes. As a result, many astronauts find it hard to get a good long sleep like they would on Earth, where there is darkness for many hours on end.

Chapter 7

HYGIENE

Astronauts do not take showers on the space station, as drops of water can fly everywhere. Instead, they use a damp cloth to wash themselves, and use only very small amounts of water to clean their teeth and wash their hair.

Clothes are washed with tiny amounts of water in a plastic bag. The clothes are dried with a special material. Any moisture then evaporates into the air and is recycled in the water recycling unit.

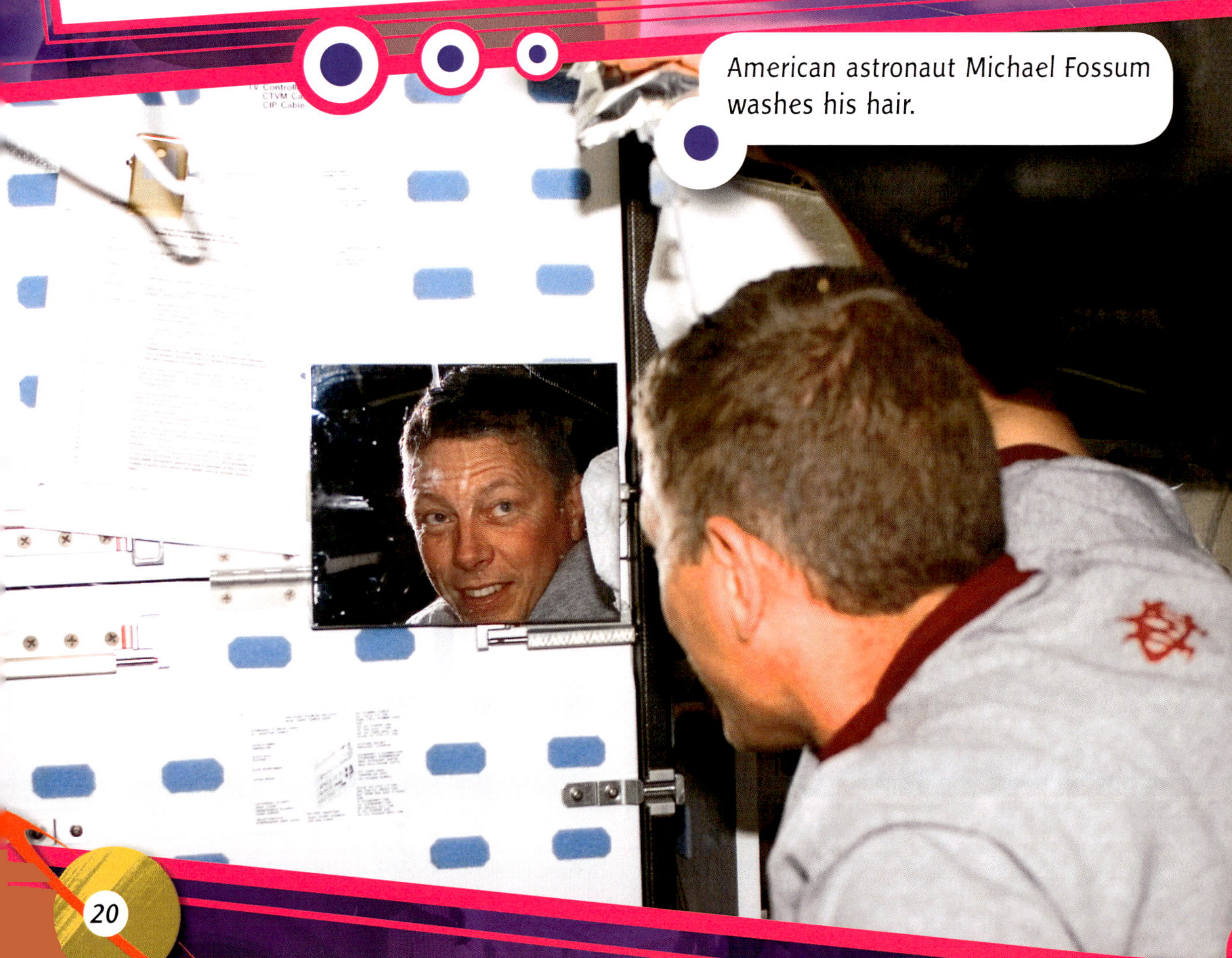

American astronaut Michael Fossum washes his hair.

Toilets on the space station have strong suction systems to stop waste floating away.

The water from human waste is also recycled in the same way as all other water on the station. Human solid waste is compacted along with other waste and sent off in a space capsule that is burnt up as it enters the Earth's atmosphere.

Chapter 8

EXERCISE

Microgravity affects astronauts' muscles and bones. The only way to make sure that muscles and bones don't waste away is for the crew to do exercises every day.

One of the biggest experiments in space has been to see how people cope with living in a microgravity environment, and how it affects their bodies.

And later ...

Even when the crews go back to Earth, they are observed closely to see how living in space has affected them. Sometimes, they are given special exercises to help make up for any bone and muscle loss from their time in space.

Glossary

dehydration the removal of water from food

canning storing food in cans

orbits goes the whole way around

Index